CW00468988

YOUR COMPLETE TAURUS 2024 PERSONAL HOROSCOPE

Monthly Astrological Prediction Forecast Readings of Every Zodiac Astrology Sun Star Signs- Love, Romance, Money, Finances, Career, Health, Travel, Spirituality.

Iris Quinn

Alpha Zuriel Publishing

Your Complete Taurus 2024 Personal Horoscope/ Iris Quinn. -
- 1st ed.

"In the dance of the planets, we find the rhythms of life. Astrology reminds us that we are all connected to the greater universe, and our actions have ripple effects throughout the cosmos."

— IRIS QUINN

CONTENTS

CHAPTER ONE

TAURUS PROFILE

Constellation: Taurus

- Zodiac symbol: Bull
- Date: April 20 - May 20
- Element: Earth
- Ruling Planet: Venus
- Career Planet: Saturn
- Love Planet: Venus
- Money Planet: Venus
- Planet of Fun, Entertainment, Creativity, and Speculations: Moon
- Planet of Health and Work: Mercury
- Planet of Home and Family Life: Venus
- Planet of Spirituality: Neptune
- Planet of Travel, Education, Religion, and Philosophy: Jupiter

Colors:
• Colors: Green, Earth tones

- Colors that promote love, romance, and social harmony: Pink, pastel shades
- Color that promotes earning power: Green

Gem: Emerald
Metals: Copper
Scent: Rose

Birthstone: Emerald

Qualities:
- Quality: Fixed (represents stability)
- Quality most needed for balance: Adaptability

Strongest Virtues:
- Patience
- Loyalty
- Practicality
- Sensuality
- Determination

Deepest Need: Security

Characteristics to Avoid:
- Stubbornness
- Possessiveness
- Resistance to change
- Over-indulgence

Signs of Greatest Overall Compatibility:
• Cancer
• Virgo
• Capricorn

Signs of Greatest Overall Incompatibility:
• Leo
• Scorpio
• Aquarius

- Sign Most Supportive for Career Advancement: Capricorn
- Sign Most Supportive for Emotional Well-being: Cancer
- Sign Most Supportive Financially: Taurus
- Sign Best for Marriage and/or Partnerships: Libra
- Sign Most Supportive for Creative Projects: Virgo
- Best Sign to Have Fun With: Pisces

Signs Most Supportive in Spiritual Matters:
• Cancer
• Scorpio
• Pisces

Best Day of the Week: Friday

TAURUS TRAITS

- Grounded and practical approach to life
- Strong sense of stability and dependability
- Appreciation for the physical world and sensory pleasures
- Patient and consistent in their actions
- Determined and persistent in pursuing their goals.
- Strong work ethic and dedication to their responsibilities
- Loyal and reliable in relationships
- Appreciation for beauty and aesthetics
- Tendency to value routine and find comfort in familiarity.
- Stubbornness and resistance to change at times.
- Strong sense of self-worth and materialistic tendencies
- Calm and composed demeanor, rarely easily angered.
- Desire for security and financial stability
- Excellent listeners and trustworthy friends

PERSONALITY OF TAURUS

Taureans, the serene guardians of existence, emanate an aura of stability and contentment. Like moss gently carpeting the forest floor, they bring a sense of grounded tranquility to the world around them. With their solid presence, they offer a reliable refuge, just like a sturdy wooden chair that provides comfort and support.

In the midst of life's chaos, Taureans stand as an oasis of peace, unwavering in their commitment to stability. Their practical nature and wealth of experience form the bedrock of their approach to life. Grounded in the physical realm, they possess a logical mindset that keeps them firmly connected to the tangible aspects of existence. They find solace in routine, as it provides them with a sense of familiarity and control. Patient and steadfast, they navigate life's ups and downs with unwavering consistency.

Breaking free from established patterns is a rare feat for Taureans, for they derive comfort and pleasure from the reliability of their routines. Like an object in motion or at rest, they prefer the serene rhythm of consistency over the unpredictable dance of chaos. Their appreciation for beauty extends beyond the

surface, as they find profound joy in the simple
pleasures of life. From savoring a favorite meal day
after day to relishing in the touch of familiar fabrics,
they elevate these experiences to a higher plane of
enjoyment.

With regal grace and unwavering determination,
Taureans are driven by a strong work ethic and a
commitment to excellence. Though they may be
perceived as stubborn and headstrong, they possess a
rare gift for listening attentively and providing
unwavering support. Like a well-crafted machine, they
can endure the tests of time, facing challenges with a
meticulous plan and unyielding resolve. They are the
dependable companions, the ones who never falter or
fail when others might crumble.

Within the realm of Taureans, stability, reliability,
and an appreciation for the physical realm coalesce to
form a personality that stands the test of time. They
embody the essence of endurance and unwavering
strength, ready to weather the storms of life with grace
and poise.

WEAKNESSES OF TAURUS

Taurus individuals, with their steadfast and grounded nature, possess a unique set of qualities that shape their personality and interactions with the world. While they have many strengths, they also face certain challenges that arise from these very qualities. Understanding these aspects allows for a more comprehensive understanding of their complexities.

One of the challenges that Taurus individuals may encounter is their inherent stubbornness. With their strong determination and unwavering will, they have a tendency to hold onto their perspectives and resist change. Once they set their sights on a goal or belief, they remain committed and resolute, refusing to be easily swayed. While this determination can be admirable, it can also hinder their ability to adapt to new situations or consider alternative viewpoints.

Possessiveness is another challenge that Taurus individuals may grapple with. Driven by their deep need for security and stability, they value what they consider theirs and can be reluctant to let go or share their resources. This possessiveness extends beyond material possessions and can also manifest in their relationships, where they may feel a strong attachment and desire for control. However, it's important for Taurus individuals to strike a balance and recognize the importance of giving their loved ones the freedom and autonomy they need.

Taurus individuals have a natural inclination towards routine and familiarity. They find comfort and security in established patterns and can be resistant to change. This resistance to change can sometimes limit their growth and hinder their ability to embrace new experiences or opportunities. However, once Taurus individuals recognize the value of stepping out of their comfort zone, they can discover new dimensions of themselves and expand their horizons.

While Taurus individuals appreciate the material world and have a keen eye for beauty and luxury, their materialistic tendencies can sometimes overshadow other aspects of life. They derive pleasure from sensory experiences and have a strong affinity for the finer things. However, it's important for them to maintain a healthy balance and not become overly fixated on material possessions, as true fulfillment comes from a holistic approach to life.

By acknowledging these potential weaknesses, Taurus individuals can navigate their personal growth journey with greater self-awareness. They can learn to embrace change, let go of possessiveness, and cultivate a more balanced approach to life. With their inherent determination, loyalty, and grounded nature, Taurus individuals have the capacity to overcome these challenges and lead fulfilling lives that are marked by stability, authenticity, and lasting relationships.

RELATIONSHIP COMPATIBILITY WITH TAURUS

Based only on their Sun signs, this is how Taurus interacts with others. These are the compatibility interpretations for all 12 potential Taurus combinations. This is a limited and insufficient method of determining compatibility.

However, Sun-sign compatibility remains the foundation for overall harmony in a relationship.

The general rule is that yin and yang do not get along. Yin complements yin, and yang complements yang. While yin and yang partnerships can be successful, they require more effort. Earth and water zodiac signs are both Yin. Yang is represented by the fire and air zodiac signs.

Taurus (Yin) and Aries (Yang)

The union between Taurus and Aries can be a combination of passion and stability. Taurus provides a grounding influence for the fiery and impulsive Aries. While Aries seeks excitement and thrills, Taurus offers a sense of security and reliability.

However, conflicts may arise due to their contrasting
approaches to life. Taurus may find Aries' impulsive
nature overwhelming, while Aries might feel
restrained by Taurus' need for routine. Finding a
balance between adventure and stability is crucial for
this relationship to thrive.

Taurus (Yin) and Taurus (Yin)

When two Taurus individuals come together, their
shared Yin energy creates a strong and stable
foundation for their relationship. They both value
security, loyalty, and the comforts of life. Their
connection is built on trust, dependability, and a deep
understanding of each other's needs. They enjoy
creating a cozy and harmonious home environment
and appreciate the simple pleasures in life. However,
they may encounter challenges when it comes to
change and adaptability. Both Taurus partners need to
be mindful of getting too comfortable or resistant to
new experiences. By embracing growth and
remaining open to new possibilities, they can cultivate
a lasting and fulfilling partnership filled with stability,
sensuality, and shared values.

Taurus (Yin) and Gemini (Yang)

Taurus and Gemini have different energies, which can create both challenges and opportunities for growth in their relationship. Taurus is grounded and practical, while Gemini is curious and adaptable. Taurus seeks stability and security, while Gemini craves variety and intellectual stimulation. Communication and understanding are vital for this pairing to succeed. Taurus can provide stability and support for Gemini's ideas, while Gemini can inspire Taurus to embrace change and broaden their horizons. Finding a balance between routine and spontaneity will be the key to a harmonious and fulfilling relationship.

Taurus (Yin) and Cancer (Yin)

Taurus and Cancer share a deep emotional connection and a desire for a loving and nurturing relationship. Both signs value stability, loyalty, and home life. Taurus brings reliability and security, while Cancer offers emotional depth and sensitivity. They create a warm and nurturing environment where they can build a strong foundation for their partnership. However, their strong attachment to the past and their resistance to change may pose challenges. Both Taurus and Cancer need to cultivate flexibility and openness to new experiences to ensure the relationship continues to evolve and grow.

Taurus (Yin) and Leo (Yang)

Taurus and Leo have contrasting energies, which can create both attraction and conflicts in their relationship. Taurus seeks stability and security, while Leo craves attention and admiration. Taurus values practicality, while Leo loves to indulge in grand gestures and displays of affection. Finding a balance between these energies is essential for the success of their partnership. Taurus can provide stability and grounding for Leo's fiery nature, while Leo can infuse excitement and passion into Taurus' life. With mutual respect and appreciation for each other's unique qualities, they can create a relationship filled with love, loyalty, and a blend of practicality and romance.

Taurus (Yin) and Virgo (Yin)

Taurus and Virgo share a practical and earthy connection, making them highly compatible. Both signs appreciate stability, loyalty, and attention to detail. They have a shared love for routine and organization, creating a harmonious and efficient partnership. Taurus offers stability and security, while Virgo brings practicality and analytical thinking. Together, they can build a solid and prosperous life based on their shared values and mutual support. However, their perfectionistic tendencies may sometimes lead to overcritical behavior. Finding balance and learning to embrace imperfections will help this relationship thrive.

Taurus (Yin) and Libra (Yang)

Taurus and Libra can create a beautiful and balanced partnership, as they complement each other's energies. Taurus seeks stability and security, while Libra values harmony and partnership. Taurus provides grounding and practicality, while Libra brings charm and diplomacy. They can create a harmonious and aesthetically pleasing home environment and appreciate the finer things in life. However, conflicts may arise due to their different approaches to decision-making. Taurus tends to be more decisive and stubborn, while Libra seeks balance and indecisiveness. Open communication and compromise are essential for maintaining a harmonious and fulfilling relationship.

Taurus (Yin) and Scorpio (Yang)

Taurus and Scorpio have a powerful and intense connection, as they share a deep emotional bond and a desire for loyalty and commitment. Taurus offers stability and reliability, while Scorpio brings passion and intensity. They have the potential for a profound and transformative partnership. However, their fixed and stubborn nature may lead to power struggles and conflicts. Both Taurus and Scorpio need to practice patience, understanding, and open communication to navigate these challenges and build a relationship based on trust, mutual support, and shared goals.

Taurus (Yin) and Sagittarius (Yang)

Taurus and Sagittarius have different energies, which can create both excitement and challenges in their relationship. Taurus seeks stability and security, while Sagittarius craves freedom and adventure. Taurus values routine and practicality, while Sagittarius loves exploration and spontaneity. Finding a balance between stability and freedom is crucial for their partnership to thrive. Taurus can provide a grounding influence for Sagittarius' restless nature, while Sagittarius can inspire Taurus to step out of their comfort zone and embrace new experiences. By respecting each other's needs and creating space for growth, they can create a relationship filled with growth, excitement, and mutual respect.

Taurus (Yin) and Capricorn (Yin)

Taurus and Capricorn share a deep connection based on their practicality, ambition, and desire for long-term security. Both signs value stability, loyalty, and hard work. Taurus provides reliability and steadfastness, while Capricorn brings determination and discipline. Together, they can create a solid and prosperous life, building a strong foundation for their shared goals. However, their serious and work-oriented nature may sometimes result in a lack of spontaneity and playfulness. Finding moments to relax and enjoy life together will help maintain a balanced and fulfilling relationship.

Taurus (Yin) and Aquarius (Yang)

Taurus and Aquarius have different energies, which can create both attraction and challenges in their relationship. Taurus seeks stability and security, while Aquarius craves freedom and independence.

Taurus values routine and tradition, while Aquarius loves innovation and unconventional thinking. Finding a balance between stability and change is crucial for their partnership to thrive. Taurus can offer grounding and support for Aquarius' ideas, while Aquarius can inspire Taurus to embrace new perspectives and ways of thinking. By celebrating their differences and fostering open-mindedness, they can create a unique and exciting relationship.

Taurus (Yin) and Pisces (Yin)

Taurus and Pisces share a deep emotional connection and a desire for a nurturing and harmonious relationship. Both signs value empathy, sensitivity, and loyalty. Taurus provides stability and security, while Pisces brings compassion and intuition. They create a safe and nurturing environment where both partners can express their emotions freely. However, their different approaches to decision-making may lead to conflicts. Taurus tends to be more practical and grounded, while Pisces relies on intuition and emotions. Finding a balance between logic and intuition is essential for maintaining a healthy and loving relationship.

LOVE AND PASSION

After overcoming the challenges that can arise in any emotional relationship, Taurus individuals are able to let down their guard and fully embrace their sensuality. They view sexual activity as a fundamental aspect of life, much like eating and drinking. As lovers, they are known for their spontaneity, generosity, and the surprising intensity of their passion. Sexual satisfaction holds great importance for them, and any dissatisfaction in this area can significantly impact their mood.

Taurus individuals have a refined taste for luxury and enjoy dressing up for special occasions and indulging in fine dining experiences. They have high standards and expect nothing but the best when it comes to experiencing pleasure. A Taurus partner can expect a life filled with sophistication, as their innate desire for pleasure extends to all aspects of their lives.

In matters of love, Taurus is a faithful and trustworthy companion. They prioritize the establishment of a solid and committed relationship above all else. They have little inclination to seek out multiple partners or engage in casual flings, as their ultimate goal is to build a lasting connection. Taurus individuals deeply value both physical and spiritual devotion from their partner, and any sense of insecurity in this area can trigger feelings of unease.

Overall, Taurus individuals bring a deep sensuality, unwavering loyalty, and a strong desire for pleasure to their intimate relationships. They thrive in an environment where their partner wholeheartedly reciprocates their commitment, both physically and spiritually. When their needs are met, Taurus becomes a passionate and devoted lover, ready to create a life of sophistication and lasting fulfillment.

MARRIAGE

Marriage holds immense significance for Taurus individuals, as they yearn for a stable and enduring bond. Their pragmatic nature leads them to carefully plan every aspect of their married life, often opting for elaborate church ceremonies to mark the solemnity of their commitment.

While some Taurus men may display possessive tendencies as the relationship progresses, it is crucial to address and curb such behavior. It is essential to foster open communication and ensure that both partners have their autonomy respected and cherished. However, beyond any possessiveness, the husband of a Taurus woman can rest assured that his spouse's unwavering loyalty and devotion are unwavering.

Taurus women are the epitome of unwavering support and unconditional love in their marriages. They wholeheartedly embrace their role as a devoted wife and are eager to create a nurturing environment for their partner. Despite starting a family, Taurus women are determined to pursue their individual passions and hobbies, which often flourish into more

than mere pastimes. Those fortunate enough to marry
a Taurus woman will be blessed with a compassionate,
dedicated, and diligent life partner.

In the realm of marriage, Taurus individuals bring
a deep sense of commitment, loyalty, and practicality.
They approach their union with a steadfast
determination to create a secure and fulfilling
relationship that withstands the test of time. With their
unwavering support, nurturing nature, and dedication
to their partner's happiness, Taurus individuals prove
to be devoted and cherished spouses, providing a solid
foundation for a harmonious and fulfilling married life.

CHAPTER TWO

TAURUS 2024 HOROSCOPE

Overview Taurus 2024

Dear Taurus, as you step into 2024, the stars align to create a year of profound growth and transformation. The planetary aspects for your sign suggest a year filled with opportunities and challenges that will shape your life in significant ways. The universe is inviting you to step out of your comfort zone and embrace the changes that are coming your way. This year, you will experience shifts in various aspects of your life, including your career, relationships, health, and personal development.

The year starts with a bit of a challenge in your professional life. In late May, Mercury in your sign forms a semi-square with Neptune in Pisces. This aspect suggests a time of potential confusion or miscommunication at work. It's a time when you need to be extra cautious with your words and decisions. Don't rush into anything without fully understanding the situation.

However, as you move into June, the planets bring more favorable conditions. Mars in your sign forms a semi-sextile with Jupiter in Gemini. This aspect indicates a time of growth and expansion in your career. You may find yourself taking on new responsibilities or pursuing new opportunities that enhance your professional standing. It's a time when your hard work starts to pay off.

In August, Mars in Gemini forms a sextile with the True Node in Aries. This aspect suggests a significant career advancement. You may find yourself in a leadership position or taking on a role that aligns with your long-term career goals. It's a time when your professional life takes a leap forward.

However, your financial life requires some caution this year. In early August, Venus in Leo squares Uranus in your sign, indicating potential financial instability. It's a time when you need to be careful with your finances and avoid impulsive spending. Make sure to plan your budget and stick to it.

In your social and personal life, 2024 brings a mix of excitement and challenges. In mid-June, Mercury in Gemini forms a semi-sextile with Uranus in your sign. This aspect suggests a time of exciting and unexpected encounters. You may meet new people who challenge your perspectives and encourage you to think differently. It's a time when your social circle expands and becomes more diverse.

However, in the same month, Venus in Gemini forms a square with Neptune in Pisces. This aspect indicates potential misunderstandings or confusion in your relationships. It's a time when communication becomes crucial. Make sure to express your feelings clearly and listen to others with an open mind.

In late June, Venus in Cancer forms a square with the True Node in Aries. This aspect suggests significant relationships entering or leaving your life. These relationships will play a crucial role in your personal growth and development. It's a time when you learn valuable lessons about love and friendship.

When it comes to your health, 2024 brings a focus on proactive care. In June, the Sun in Gemini forms a semi-sextile with Uranus in your sign. This aspect suggests a time of unexpected changes in your health. It's a time when you need to be proactive in taking care of your physical well-being. Regular check-ups and a balanced diet become more important than ever.

In August, the Sun in Leo forms a trine with the True Node in Aries. This aspect indicates a time of vitality and good health. It's a time when you feel energetic and full of life. Use this time to focus on your wellness goals and implement healthy habits into your daily routine.

2024 is a significant year for your spiritual growth and personal development. In May, Jupiter in Gemini forms a quintile with Saturn in Pisces, suggesting a time of spiritual awakening and growth. You may find yourself drawn to spiritual practices or philosophies that enhance your understanding of the universe and your place in it. This is a time for introspection and self-discovery, where you might find a deeper sense of purpose and meaning in your life.

In December, the Sun in Sagittarius forms a quincunx with Uranus in your sign. This aspect indicates a time of sudden insights and revelations. These insights may challenge your current beliefs and encourage you to explore new perspectives. This is a time of transformation, where you might find yourself questioning old beliefs and opening up to new ideas and philosophies.

Throughout 2024, the planets encourage you to focus on personal development. The semi-sextile between Mars in Taurus and Jupiter in Gemini in June suggests a time of learning and expanding your skills. This is a great time to take up a new hobby or learn something new that can contribute to your personal growth.

In August, Venus in Leo squares Uranus in Taurus, indicating a time of self-reflection. You might find yourself questioning your values and what truly matters to you. This is a time to reassess your priorities and make changes that align with your true self.

Dear Taurus, 2024 is a year of transformation and growth. The planetary aspects suggest that this year will be a journey of self-discovery and personal development. You will face challenges, but remember, these challenges are opportunities for growth. Embrace the changes and let them guide you towards your highest potential. Stay grounded, embrace your resilience, and trust in the journey. This is your year to shine, Taurus. Embrace it with open arms and an open heart.

January 2024

Horoscope

January brings a mix of celestial influences for
Taurus, creating a dynamic and eventful month. As
the year begins, on January 1st, Venus forms a square
aspect with Saturn, indicating a potential clash
between your desire for adventure and the need for
stability. It's important to find a balance between
exploring new horizons and maintaining a solid
foundation in your life.

On January 3rd, Venus forms a quincunx aspect with
Jupiter, suggesting that adjustments may be necessary
in matters of love and relationships. You may feel
torn between different desires or find it challenging to
align your personal values with the dynamics of your
partnerships. It's a time for reflection and finding
harmony between your individual needs and the
expectations of others.

Mercury's quintile with Saturn on January 3rd
enhances your intellectual abilities and encourages
practical thinking. This aspect supports your
communication skills and helps you find practical
solutions to any challenges that arise.

Throughout the month, there are several planetary
interactions that highlight the importance of balancing
your personal desires with your social connections.
The Sun's square aspect with Chiron on January 6th
suggests a need for healing and growth in your self-
expression and confidence. Embrace the opportunity
to address any insecurities and tap into your inner
strength.

In the realm of career and professional pursuits, the
trine between the Sun and Uranus on January 9th
brings innovative and unexpected opportunities. You
may find yourself drawn to unique projects or ideas
that have the potential to propel your career forward.
Mars' favorable aspects with Saturn and Jupiter on
January 9th and 12th, respectively, provide the drive
and ambition needed to make significant progress in
your professional endeavors.

Love

In matters of the heart, January brings a blend of harmonious and challenging energies for Taurus. The quincunx aspect between Venus and Jupiter on January 3rd may bring some adjustments or compromises in your relationships. You might need to reassess your values and expectations to find a better alignment with your partner's needs.

On January 11th, Venus forms a trine with Chiron, offering opportunities for deep emotional healing within your relationships. This aspect encourages open communication and the willingness to address any emotional wounds or past traumas that may be affecting your love life. It's a favorable time for understanding and supporting each other's vulnerabilities.

Throughout the month, Taurus can expect romantic surprises and unexpected connections, thanks to Venus' biquintile aspect with Jupiter and Uranus on January 8th and 19th, respectively. These aspects bring excitement and novelty into your love life, offering new perspectives and the potential for passionate encounters.

For those who are single, January presents opportunities to meet new people and explore different romantic possibilities. However, it's important to approach these encounters with a discerning eye, as Venus' square aspect with Neptune on January 19th may create some confusion or illusions in matters of the heart. Take your time to get to know someone before diving into a committed relationship.

Career

January holds promising energies for Taurus in terms of career and professional growth. The trine aspect between Mars and Jupiter on January 12th empowers you with the ambition, drive, and confidence to pursue your career goals. You may find yourself taking the initiative to expand your professional network, seek new opportunities, or showcase your skills and talents.

Saturn's supportive aspects with Mars and Uranus on January 9th and 19th, respectively, add stability and structure to your career endeavors. This is a favorable time to lay a solid foundation for long-term success, whether through meticulous planning, disciplined work ethic, or seeking guidance from mentors or experts in your field.

The conjunction between the Sun and Pluto on January 20th highlights a transformative period in your professional life. You may experience a shift in your ambitions, a change in your career path, or a deep dive into personal growth and empowerment. Embrace this transformative energy and use it to make positive changes in your professional life.

Throughout the month, communication and collaboration play crucial roles in your career success. Mercury's square aspect with Neptune on January 8th may introduce some confusion or miscommunication in the workplace. It's important to double-check details, clarify expectations, and maintain open lines of communication to avoid misunderstandings.

Taurus professionals may find themselves drawn to innovative and unconventional projects or ideas, thanks to Mercury's trine with Uranus on January 19th. Embrace your creative thinking and willingness to step outside of traditional boundaries. This aspect can lead to exciting breakthroughs and unique solutions in your professional endeavors.

Finance

Taurus individuals can expect a mixed financial outlook in January. The square aspect between Venus and Saturn on January 1st suggests the need for caution and prudence when it comes to money matters. It's essential to stick to a budget, avoid impulsive spending, and focus on long-term financial stability rather than immediate gratification.

On January 8th, Venus' biquintile aspect with Jupiter brings opportunities for financial growth and abundance. You may receive unexpected financial rewards or find luck in speculative ventures. However, it's important to exercise moderation and avoid excessive risk-taking. Maintain a balanced approach to financial decisions and consider seeking professional advice when needed.

Throughout the month, maintaining a clear and realistic perspective on your financial situation is crucial. Mercury's square aspect with Neptune on January 8th may create confusion or unrealistic expectations regarding money matters. Be cautious when making financial agreements or investments, and ensure that you have a thorough understanding of the terms and conditions involved.

The trine aspect between Venus and Chiron on January 11th encourages you to address any emotional or psychological factors that may be influencing your financial decisions. Consider seeking financial counseling or exploring your beliefs and attitudes towards money to achieve a healthier relationship with your finances.

Practicality and discipline are essential for financial success in January. Saturn's semi-square aspect with True Node on January 15th reinforces the importance of long-term planning and making responsible financial choices. Focus on building a strong financial foundation and consider long-term investments that align with your goals and values.

Health

January brings a focus on physical and emotional well-being for Taurus. With the Sun's square aspect to Chiron on January 6th, it's essential to pay attention to any physical or emotional wounds that may need healing. Take time for self-care, engage in activities that nurture your body and soul, and seek support if needed.

Maintaining a balanced routine is key to your overall health and well-being. The semi-square aspect between the Sun and Saturn on January 9th emphasizes the need for discipline and structure in your daily habits. Consider implementing a regular exercise routine, ensuring sufficient rest and relaxation, and maintaining a nutritious diet.

The trine aspect between Mars and Jupiter on January 12th brings a boost of energy and motivation. Use this dynamic energy to engage in physical activities that you enjoy, such as sports, yoga, or dance. Regular exercise not only benefits your physical health but also enhances your mental and emotional well-being.

Taurus individuals may also find it beneficial to explore alternative healing modalities or holistic approaches to health. The quintile aspect between Mars and Neptune on January 22nd supports the integration of mind, body, and spirit. Consider practices such as meditation, energy healing, or mindfulness to promote balance and inner harmony.

Emotional well-being is equally important, and the trine aspect between Venus and Chiron on January 11th offers opportunities for emotional healing and self-care. Take time for self-reflection, express your emotions in healthy ways, and seek support from loved ones or professionals if needed.

To maintain optimal health, it's important to prioritize stress management and relaxation techniques. The quintile aspect between Mercury and Neptune on January 24th enhances your intuitive abilities and encourages practices such as journaling, art therapy, or engaging with nature to promote inner peace and reduce stress.

Travel

January presents opportunities for travel and exploration for Taurus individuals. The semi-sextile aspect between Uranus and the True Node on January 23rd introduces unexpected and spontaneous travel opportunities. You may find yourself drawn to new experiences or encounter unplanned trips that offer unique adventures.

When planning your travels, it's important to maintain flexibility and adaptability. The semi-sextile aspect between Venus and Uranus on January 14th suggests that unexpected changes may occur during your journeys. Embrace these surprises as opportunities for growth and new discoveries.

Taurus individuals may also find joy in reconnecting with nature or exploring destinations that offer peace and tranquility. The sextile aspect between the Sun and Neptune on January 15th enhances your connection with the natural world and encourages retreats or vacations that promote relaxation and spiritual rejuvenation.

When traveling, it's essential to prioritize self-care and well-being. The square aspect between the Sun and Jupiter on January 27th may create a tendency to overindulge or take risks. Ensure that you maintain a balanced approach to your travel experiences, including maintaining a healthy diet, getting enough rest, and staying within your budget.

Consider exploring destinations that align with your personal interests and desires. The trine aspect between Venus and Jupiter on January 8th enhances your appreciation for culture, art, and beauty. Plan trips that allow you to indulge in the arts, visit museums, or immerse yourself in the local cuisine.

Throughout your travels, embrace the opportunity to expand your horizons, learn from different cultures, and connect with new people. The quintile aspect between Mars and Neptune on January 22nd enhances your sense of adventure and encourages interactions with locals or engaging in meaningful experiences that broaden your perspectives.

Insight from the Stars

January is a month of duality for Taurus - it's a time
for action but also reflection. The stars favor your
ambitions, but the retrograde calls for caution. Utilize
the grounded Capricorn energy to lay the foundation
for the year ahead but be adaptable to the twists and
turns that the retrograde might bring.

Best days of the month: January 9th, 11th, 12th, 15th,
19th, 22nd, and 28th

February 2024

Horoscope

In February, Taurus individuals will experience a blend of transformative energies and opportunities for self-reflection. The month begins with Mars forming a semi-square aspect with Saturn on February 2nd, indicating potential challenges in asserting yourself and taking decisive action. It's important to exercise patience and avoid impulsive reactions. Focus on finding a balance between ambition and practicality.

As the month progresses, Taurus individuals will feel a surge of intellectual energy and creativity. Mercury's sextile aspect with Neptune on February 5th enhances your intuitive abilities and stimulates imaginative thinking. This is an excellent time for introspection, creative pursuits, and exploring new ideas.

Taurus individuals may find opportunities for spiritual growth and introspection in February. The conjunction between the Sun and Neptune on February 15th heightens your intuition and connection with the higher realms. Engage in practices such as meditation, journaling, or engaging with nature to enhance your spiritual well-being.

Overall, February encourages Taurus individuals to embrace self-reflection, prioritize healing and growth in relationships, exercise financial discipline, maintain physical and emotional well-being, and embark on meaningful travel experiences. By embracing these aspects, Taurus individuals can navigate the month with grace, personal development, and a deeper connection with their inner selves.

Love

In matters of the heart, February brings opportunities for healing, growth, and increased emotional connection for Taurus individuals. The square aspect between Venus and Chiron on February 5th may bring emotional wounds or insecurities to the surface. It's essential to address these issues within your

relationships and create a safe space for open and
honest communication.

The sextile aspect between the Sun and Chiron on the
same day offers a chance for emotional healing and
growth. This aspect encourages vulnerability and
understanding, allowing you to work through past
hurts and deepen the emotional bond with your
partner. Single Taurus individuals may find that this
energy opens doors to new connections based on
authenticity and shared emotional depth.

Throughout the month, it's important to maintain a
balance between your individual needs and the
expectations of your partner. The conjunction
between Venus and Mars on February 22nd brings a
blend of passion and assertiveness to your
relationships. Embrace this dynamic energy but
remember to communicate your desires and listen to
the needs of your partner.

For single Taurus individuals, February offers
opportunities for new romantic encounters. The
sextile aspect between Venus and True Node on
February 29th enhances your magnetism and
increases the chances of meeting someone who aligns
with your long-term goals and values.

Career

February presents transformative energies and significant opportunities for Taurus individuals in their professional lives. The conjunction between Mercury and Pluto on February 5th enhances your analytical abilities and deepens your understanding of complex issues. Use this transformative energy to make strategic decisions, engage in meaningful work, and seek opportunities for professional growth.

Throughout the month, communication and networking play crucial roles in your career success. The sextile aspect between Mercury and Chiron on February 15th enhances your communication skills and encourages you to express your ideas and opinions with confidence. Take advantage of networking events or engage in conversations that promote collaboration and learning.

Financial matters require careful consideration in February. The semi-square aspect between Venus and Saturn on February 10th reminds you of the importance of financial discipline and responsibility. It's crucial to create a realistic budget, monitor your expenses, and make informed decisions regarding investments or financial commitments.

Taurus individuals may experience a period of empowerment and recognition in their professional endeavors. The quintile aspect between Mercury and Jupiter on February 22nd enhances your creativity, problem-solving abilities, and enthusiasm for your work. This is a favorable time to take on new projects, seek promotions, or explore entrepreneurial opportunities.

Collaboration and teamwork are highlighted in February, thanks to the quintile aspect between Mercury and Uranus on February 27th. Embrace innovative ideas, be open to feedback, and seek out diverse perspectives. This collaborative energy can lead to breakthroughs and creative solutions in your career.

Finance

In February, Taurus individuals are advised to approach their finances with discipline, caution, and a long-term perspective. The semi-square aspect between Venus and Saturn on February 10th serves as a reminder of the importance of financial responsibility. This aspect calls for budgeting, sticking to a financial plan, and avoiding impulsive spending.

It's crucial to strike a balance between financial stability and the pursuit of your desires. The conjunction between Venus and Mars on February 22nd brings a blend of passion and assertiveness, which can sometimes lead to impulsive financial decisions. Be mindful of your financial goals and consider the long-term impact of your choices.

Throughout the month, it's important to seek financial advice when needed. The quintile aspect between Mercury and Jupiter on February 22nd enhances your analytical abilities and decision-making skills. Consider consulting with financial experts, engaging in research, or seeking professional advice to make informed financial choices.

The semi-square aspect between Mercury and Neptune on February 12th reminds Taurus individuals to remain cautious and discerning in financial matters. Be mindful of potential scams or unrealistic promises regarding financial investments or opportunities. Do thorough research and rely on trusted sources before making any significant financial commitments.

Opportunities for financial growth and unexpected gains may arise in February. The sextile aspect between Venus and Uranus on February 7th opens doors to innovative financial ventures or unexpected windfalls. However, it's essential to exercise moderation and avoid excessive risk-taking. Balance your desire for financial growth with responsible decision-making and long-term stability.

Health

The semi-square aspect between Mars and Saturn on February 2nd may introduce challenges in maintaining your physical well-being. It's crucial to practice patience, listen to your body, and avoid pushing yourself too hard. Embrace a balanced approach to physical activities, combining exercise with rest and relaxation.

Emotional well-being is equally important for Taurus individuals in February. The semi-square aspect between Mars and Neptune on February 7th emphasizes the need to set healthy boundaries and practice self-care. Engage in activities that nurture your emotional health, such as journaling, meditation, or spending time in nature.

Maintaining a healthy diet and nutrition is crucial for overall well-being. The sextile aspect between Venus and Neptune on February 13th encourages you to explore new recipes, embrace nourishing foods, and seek pleasure in the culinary arts. Pay attention to your body's needs and aim for a balanced and nutritious diet.

February invites Taurus individuals to engage in spiritual practices that promote inner peace and well-being. The conjunction between the Sun and Neptune on February 15th enhances your intuitive abilities and connection with the spiritual realm. Embrace practices such as meditation, yoga, or energy healing to promote balance and harmony within yourself.

Stress management is crucial in maintaining optimal health. The quintile aspect between the Sun and Uranus on February 26th encourages you to explore new stress-relief techniques and find what works best for you. Consider practices such as mindfulness, deep breathing exercises, or engaging in hobbies that bring you joy.

Travel

In February, Taurus individuals may experience opportunities for travel and exploration. The quintile aspect between Mercury and Jupiter on February 22nd enhances your sense of adventure, curiosity, and desire to explore new horizons.

When planning your travels, it's important to embrace flexibility and adaptability. The semi-square aspect between Venus and Saturn on February 10th suggests that unexpected changes may occur during your journeys. Be open to adjusting your plans and embrace these surprises as opportunities for growth and new experiences.

Consider exploring destinations that offer a blend of cultural richness and natural beauty. The sextile aspect between Venus and True Node on February 29th enhances your appreciation for unique experiences and connections with locals. Engage in cultural activities, try local cuisines, and immerse yourself in the traditions of the places you visit.

February also encourages Taurus individuals to embark on inner journeys and spiritual retreats. The conjunction between the Sun and Neptune on February 15th enhances your connection with the spiritual realm and promotes introspection. Consider retreats that offer opportunities for meditation, self-reflection, and connecting with nature.

When traveling, be mindful of your physical and emotional well-being. The semi-square aspect between Mars and Neptune on February 28th emphasizes the need to set boundaries and practice self-care. Ensure that you prioritize rest, engage in activities that nurture your body and soul, and practice stress management techniques.

Insight from the stars

February is a month of duality – the need for innovation and stability, social expansion and introspection. It's a month to embrace your uniqueness, but also to stay true to your Taurus roots.

Best days of the month: February 2nd, 5th, 10th, 15th, 22nd, 26th, and 29th

March 2024

Horoscope

In March, Taurus individuals will experience a blend of transformative energies, spiritual exploration, and opportunities for personal growth. This month invites you to embrace change, tap into your intuitive abilities, and cultivate a deeper connection with your inner self.

The sextile aspect between the Sun and Jupiter on March 1st brings optimism, expansion, and a renewed sense of purpose. This aspect encourages you to explore new horizons, set ambitious goals, and embrace opportunities for personal and spiritual growth.

Throughout March, you may find yourself drawn to spiritual practices and introspection. The conjunction between the Sun and Neptune on March 17th enhances your intuitive abilities and promotes a deeper connection with the spiritual realm. Embrace practices such as meditation, journaling, or energy healing to enhance your spiritual journey.

Overall, March encourages Taurus individuals to embrace change, nurture their spiritual well-being, navigate relationships with adaptability, focus on professional growth, practice financial responsibility, prioritize health and self-care, and embrace opportunities for travel and adventure.

Love

The square aspect between Venus and Uranus on March 3rd may bring unexpected changes or disruptions in established relationships. This aspect serves as a catalyst for growth and encourages you to embrace new experiences and perspectives.

For single Taurus individuals, March presents opportunities for exciting romantic encounters. The sextile aspect between Venus and Chiron on March 6th enhances your magnetism and increases the chances of meeting someone who appreciates your unique qualities. Embrace your vulnerability, be open to new connections, and trust your instincts when it comes to matters of the heart.

The conjunction between Venus and Saturn on March 21st highlights the importance of commitment and long-term compatibility in romantic relationships. This aspect encourages you to take your time, build a solid foundation, and ensure that your values align with those of your partner. Patience and understanding will be key as you navigate the complexities of love.

In established relationships, communication and compromise are crucial in maintaining harmony. The semi-square aspect between Venus and Pluto on March 12th may bring intense emotions or power struggles. It's important to approach conflicts with empathy, actively listen to your partner's perspective, and find mutually beneficial solutions.

Emotional healing and growth can be achieved through open and honest communication. The conjunction between Mercury and Chiron on March 20th supports healing conversations and encourages vulnerability with your partner. Share your deepest fears, desires, and dreams, allowing for a deeper connection and mutual understanding.

Career

The semi-sextile aspect between Mercury and Saturn on March 16th emphasizes the need for focused effort, discipline, and attention to detail in your career.

This month, it's important to take responsibility for your professional development. Seek opportunities to refine your skills, expand your knowledge, and stay updated on industry trends. This will enhance your expertise and contribute to your long-term success.

Networking and collaboration play a significant role in your career advancement. The semi-square aspect between Mercury and Mars on March 14th highlights the importance of assertiveness and effective communication in professional relationships. Embrace opportunities to connect with colleagues, share your ideas, and collaborate on projects.

Maintaining a professional image and reputation is essential. The conjunction between Venus and Saturn on March 21st encourages you to uphold high standards of professionalism, integrity, and reliability. Be consistent in your work, meet deadlines, and demonstrate your commitment to excellence.

Financial stability and responsibility should be a focus in your career endeavors. The semi-square aspect between Venus and Pluto on March 12th reminds you to be cautious in financial matters. Avoid impulsive decisions and seek expert advice when necessary. Long-term financial planning and budgeting will contribute to your overall professional success.

March also presents opportunities for leadership and taking on new responsibilities. The conjunction between Mercury and the True Node on March 18th enhances your influence and encourages you to step into positions of authority. Embrace these opportunities with confidence and utilize your natural leadership abilities to make a positive impact.

Finance

In March, Taurus individuals are encouraged to approach their finances with caution, responsibility, and long-term planning. The conjunction between Venus and Saturn on March 21st reminds you of the importance of financial stability and wise financial decisions.

It's crucial to review your budget, assess your expenses, and make necessary adjustments to ensure that you're living within your means. Cut back on unnecessary expenses and prioritize essential financial commitments.

Long-term financial planning is essential for your future security. Consider consulting with a financial advisor who can guide you in making informed decisions about investments, savings, and retirement planning. Take advantage of the knowledge and expertise available to you.

While it's important to save for the future, it's also essential to find a balance and enjoy the present. The semi-square aspect between Venus and Pluto on March 12th reminds you to find pleasure in the simple things without overspending. Seek joy in experiences that don't necessarily require significant financial investment, such as spending quality time with loved ones or engaging in hobbies that bring you fulfillment.

Avoid impulsive or risky financial decisions. The semi-square aspect between Mercury and Uranus on March 12th reminds you to be cautious and think through potential risks before making any major financial commitments. Patience and thorough analysis will protect you from unnecessary financial setbacks.

Health

In March, Taurus individuals are encouraged to prioritize their health and well-being. The conjunction between Mercury and Chiron on March 20th brings opportunities for emotional healing and self-care.

Emotional well-being is crucial for overall health. Take time for self-reflection, engage in activities that bring you joy, and seek support from loved ones or a therapist if needed. Prioritize your mental and emotional health, as they play a significant role in your overall well-being.

Maintaining a balanced lifestyle is essential. The semi-square aspect between Venus and Pluto on March 12th reminds you to avoid extremes and find moderation in your habits. Focus on maintaining a healthy diet, regular exercise routine, and sufficient sleep. Embrace practices such as meditation or yoga to promote inner peace and reduce stress.

Stress management is crucial in March. The semi-square aspect between Mercury and Mars on March 14th may bring moments of tension or restlessness. Engage in stress-relieving activities such as deep breathing exercises, journaling, or engaging in hobbies that bring you relaxation. Find healthy outlets to release pent-up energy and maintain a sense of calm.

It's essential to listen to your body's needs and address any physical discomfort or ailments. Regular check-ups with healthcare professionals are encouraged, as prevention and early detection are key in maintaining optimal health.

Nurturing your spiritual well-being can positively impact your overall health. The conjunction between the Sun and Neptune on March 17th enhances your intuitive abilities and connection to the spiritual realm. Engage in practices such as meditation, mindfulness, or prayer to enhance your spiritual journey and find inner peace.

Travel

The quintile aspect between Venus and Uranus on March 18th ignites your sense of adventure and encourages you to embrace new experiences and destinations.

When planning your travels, seek destinations that offer cultural enrichment, natural beauty, and spiritual growth. Embrace flexibility in your itinerary and allow for spontaneity, as unexpected opportunities may arise.

Consider engaging in activities such as yoga retreats, meditation workshops, or nature-focused adventures. These experiences will not only provide physical rejuvenation but also contribute to your personal growth and self-discovery.

Embrace solo travel or group experiences that allow you to connect with like-minded individuals. Seek out opportunities to engage with local communities, immerse yourself in different cultures, and broaden your perspectives.

March encourages Taurus individuals to prioritize their well-being during their travels. Take time for self-care, prioritize rest and relaxation, and engage in activities that promote inner peace and rejuvenation. Find a balance between exploration and rejuvenation to make the most of your travel experiences.

Nature-focused destinations can provide a sense of grounding and connection. Consider visiting serene landscapes, national parks, or coastal areas that allow you to reconnect with the natural world and find solace in its beauty.

Incorporate spiritual practices into your travel
experiences. Visit sacred sites, engage in meditation
or mindfulness practices, or seek out spiritual teachers
or guides who can deepen your spiritual journey.

Remember to prioritize safety during your travels.
Stay informed about local customs, follow guidelines
and regulations, and take necessary precautions to
ensure a smooth and secure journey.

Insight from the stars

The stars in March are aligning to bring about
personal transformation. Through Pisces, they
whisper dreams and intuition, and through Aries, they
shout action and ambition. It's a month to dream, act,
and transform.

Best days of the month: March 1st, 6th, 17th, 18th,
21st, 24th and 26th.

April 2024

Horoscope

April brings a mix of energy for Taurus individuals, with opportunities for growth, self-reflection, and the need to adapt to changing circumstances. The month begins with the semi-sextile aspect between Mercury and Venus on April 2nd, encouraging harmonious communication and social interactions. It's an ideal time to connect with loved ones, express your thoughts, and engage in meaningful conversations.

The Sun's semi-sextile aspect with Saturn on April 2nd reminds Taurus individuals to maintain a balanced approach to responsibilities and commitments. Finding a harmonious balance between work and personal life is crucial during this period.

On April 3rd, the Sun forms a quintile aspect with Pluto, bringing an opportunity for self-transformation and empowerment. Embrace your inner strength and utilize it to overcome challenges and make positive changes in your life.

Mars and Uranus form a quintile aspect on April 3rd, infusing you with innovative and adventurous energy. It's a time to embrace your spontaneous side, explore new experiences, and take calculated risks.

Maintaining effective communication becomes essential as Mercury semi-squares Mars on April 6th. Be mindful of conflicts or impulsive reactions, and focus on finding diplomatic solutions in your interactions.

The sextile aspect between Venus and Pluto on April 6th intensifies your romantic and emotional connections. It's a favorable time for deepening relationships and exploring the depths of your desires.

The semi-sextile aspect between the Sun and Jupiter on April 8th brings a boost of confidence and optimism. This alignment supports your endeavors, especially in the realms of personal growth and career advancement.

The conjunction between the Sun and Chiron on April 8th invites you to embrace your vulnerabilities and engage in healing activities. This alignment brings opportunities for emotional healing and self-discovery, allowing you to release old wounds and embrace a renewed sense of self.

Love

In love, April presents both challenges and opportunities for Taurus individuals. The conjunction between Venus and Chiron on April 21st highlights the need for healing and growth in relationships. It's a time to confront past hurts, release emotional baggage, and embrace vulnerability to foster deeper connections.

Communication plays a vital role in nurturing love during this period. Mercury's conjunction with Venus on April 19th enhances your ability to express your feelings and desires with clarity and sincerity. Use this time to have open and honest conversations with your partner, addressing any unresolved issues and fostering greater understanding.

Taurus individuals may feel a strong desire for stability and security in their relationships. The semi-sextile aspect between Venus and Saturn on April 17th encourages you to invest in long-term commitments and build a solid foundation of trust and loyalty. Take time to assess the strength of your relationships and make necessary adjustments to enhance stability and harmony.

The semi-square aspect between Venus and Jupiter on April 8th reminds you to maintain a balanced approach to love. Avoid excessive expectations or overindulgence, as it may lead to disappointment or conflicts. Instead, focus on nurturing your connections through genuine care, compassion, and quality time together.

For single Taurus individuals, the conjunction between Venus and Neptune on April 3rd infuses your romantic life with a touch of magic and enchantment. You may find yourself drawn to dreamy and imaginative partners. However, be cautious of idealizing others too much and maintain a grounded perspective to ensure compatibility and long-term fulfillment.

Career

The semi-sextile aspect between Mercury and Venus on April 2nd enhances your communication skills and allows you to express your ideas with clarity and charm. This is an excellent time to present your proposals, engage in negotiations, or share your creative insights with colleagues and superiors.

The Sun's semi-sextile aspect with Saturn on April 2nd reminds Taurus individuals to maintain a disciplined and responsible approach to their work. Focus on meeting deadlines, fulfilling your obligations, and demonstrating reliability. Your diligent efforts will be recognized and rewarded, paving the way for long-term success.

On April 8th, the semi-sextile aspect between the Sun and Jupiter brings opportunities for career expansion and growth. Embrace new challenges, take calculated risks, and trust in your abilities to achieve professional success. This alignment also encourages you to seek out mentors or educational opportunities that can further enhance your skills and knowledge.

The conjunction between the Sun and Chiron on April 8th invites Taurus individuals to address any limiting beliefs or self-doubt that may hinder their career progress. Use this time for introspection and personal

growth, as healing past wounds can unlock your full
potential and allow you to step into positions of
leadership and influence.

Maintaining effective communication becomes
crucial as Mercury semi-squares Mars on April 6th.
Be mindful of conflicts or misunderstandings in your
workplace and strive to find diplomatic solutions.
Practice active listening and constructive dialogue to
maintain harmonious relationships with colleagues
and superiors.

The sextile aspect between Venus and Pluto on April
6th ignites your passion and determination in
pursuing your career goals. This alignment empowers
you to make transformative changes and assert your
influence within your professional sphere. Use this
energy to embrace new challenges, take on leadership
roles, and showcase your talents.

Taurus individuals may also benefit from networking
and forming alliances during April. The semi-sextile
aspect between Venus and Mars on April 27th
encourages collaboration and teamwork. Seek out
opportunities to connect with like-minded individuals
or industry peers who can support your professional
aspirations.

Finance

The semi-square aspect between Venus and Saturn on April 17th cautions against impulsive spending or indulging in luxury without considering the long-term consequences. It's essential to maintain a balanced and disciplined approach to your finances during this time. Create a budget, prioritize your expenses, and focus on building a solid foundation for financial stability.

On April 9th, the semi-square aspect between the Sun and Jupiter reminds Taurus individuals to avoid excessive risk-taking or overconfidence in financial matters. Take a cautious and measured approach when making investment decisions or engaging in financial ventures. Seeking advice from trusted financial advisors or professionals can provide valuable insights and help you make sound choices.

The conjunction between Venus and Neptune on April 3rd highlights the importance of financial discernment. Be wary of potential illusions or deceptive financial schemes. Ensure that you thoroughly research and analyze any investment opportunities before committing your resources. Trust your intuition and listen to your inner voice when making financial decisions.

The semi-sextile aspect between Venus and Mars on April 27th brings opportunities for financial collaborations or joint ventures. Consider partnering with reliable individuals who share your financial goals and values. Together, you can pool your resources and leverage each other's strengths to achieve mutual financial success.

Taurus individuals may also benefit from exploring alternative sources of income during April. The semi-sextile aspect between Mercury and Uranus on April 21st encourages innovative thinking and a willingness to explore unconventional financial avenues. Stay open to new ideas, embrace your entrepreneurial spirit, and consider diversifying your income streams.

Maintaining financial discipline and avoiding impulsive spending is crucial throughout April. Create a savings plan, practice mindful spending, and prioritize financial security. This will provide a solid foundation for long-term financial prosperity and peace of mind.

Remember that financial well-being is closely tied to your overall sense of stability and security. Use this month to cultivate a healthy relationship with money, balance your material desires with practicality, and focus on long-term financial goals. By adopting a disciplined and mindful approach, you can pave the way for financial abundance and security in the future.

Health

The semi-sextile aspect between Mars and Chiron on April 11th draws attention to the importance of addressing any lingering health issues or discomfort. Don't ignore subtle signs from your body. Take proactive steps to address any physical ailments or seek professional advice if needed. This is a favorable time for healing and seeking alternative therapies or holistic approaches to improve your overall well-being.

The conjunction between Venus and Chiron on April 21st emphasizes the connection between emotional and physical health. Pay attention to your emotional state and take steps to nurture your mental and emotional well-being. Engage in activities that bring you joy, practice self-care rituals, and seek support from loved ones or professionals if you're experiencing emotional challenges.

Maintaining a balanced and nutritious diet is essential for your health during April. The semi-square aspect between Venus and Saturn on April 30th reminds you to make conscious choices when it comes to your diet. Be mindful of indulging in unhealthy or comfort foods. Focus on incorporating nutrient-rich foods into your meals, staying hydrated, and maintaining a consistent exercise routine.

The sextile aspect between Mars and Jupiter on April 19th encourages physical activity and a proactive approach to fitness. Engage in exercises or activities that bring you pleasure and help release any pent-up energy or stress. Consider exploring new workout routines or joining group classes to keep your fitness journey exciting and motivating.

April is also a favorable time for relaxation and self-care practices. The conjunction between the Sun and Mercury on April 11th supports taking breaks and finding moments of calm amidst a busy schedule. Incorporate mindfulness exercises, meditation, or other relaxation techniques into your daily routine to promote a sense of inner peace and reduce stress.

Travel

The semi-square aspect between Venus and Saturn on April 17th suggests the need for careful planning and preparation before embarking on any trips. Double-check travel itineraries, ensure you have all the necessary documents and accommodations booked in advance. Pay attention to travel advisories and be prepared for any unexpected changes or delays that may arise.

The conjunction between the Sun and Mercury on April 11th encourages communication and gathering information about potential travel destinations. Research thoroughly, read reviews, and seek recommendations to make informed decisions about where to go and what to do during your travels. Engage in conversations with fellow travelers or locals to gain valuable insights and enhance your overall travel experience.

April is a favorable time for travel experiences that focus on self-discovery and personal growth. The semi-sextile aspect between Mars and Chiron on April 13th supports engaging in activities or retreats that promote inner healing and spiritual development. Consider destinations known for their serene and peaceful environments, such as nature retreats or wellness resorts. These experiences can provide a deeper sense of rejuvenation and self-reflection.

The semi-sextile aspect between Venus and Jupiter on April 22nd amplifies the potential for enjoying luxurious and indulgent travel experiences. Treat yourself to a well-deserved vacation where you can immerse yourself in comfort and relaxation. Whether it's a spa retreat, beach getaway, or cultural excursion, allow yourself to fully embrace the pleasures and experiences that travel has to offer.

However, it's important to remain flexible and adaptable during your travels, as the semi-square aspect between Venus and Mars on April 27th may bring some unexpected challenges or conflicts. Stay patient and open-minded, and be willing to adjust your plans if necessary. Embrace the spirit of adventure and see any detours or changes as opportunities for growth and new experiences.

Insight from the stars

"Just as stars shine brightest in the darkest nights, your resilience shines through adversity. Keep shining, Taurus." - The stars acknowledge Taurus' innate resilience and remind them to keep persevering through challenging times, knowing that their light will continue to shine.

Best days of the month: April 2nd, 8th, 10th, 16th, 19th, 22nd, and 30th.

May 2024

Horoscope

May brings a mix of energies for Taurus, with opportunities for growth, challenges to overcome, and moments of self-reflection. The month begins with Venus square Pluto, creating tension in relationships. It's essential to address any underlying issues and communicate openly to maintain harmony.

Mars sextile Pluto on May 3rd brings determination and power to pursue your goals. Use this energy to make progress in your career or personal projects. However, be mindful of potential power struggles or conflicts, as Mars can be intense.

On May 6th, the Sun semi-square Neptune may create some confusion or a need to escape reality. Take time for self-care and reflection to find clarity and recharge. Embrace spirituality or creative pursuits to find inspiration.

The alignment between the Sun and the True Node on May 5th and 11th encourages self-discovery and aligning with your true purpose. These moments offer a chance to reflect on your values, aspirations, and direction in life.

May 18th is a significant day with Venus conjunct Uranus and the Sun conjunct Jupiter. This powerful combination brings excitement, unexpected opportunities, and a desire for freedom. Embrace new experiences and explore uncharted territories. However, be cautious not to be impulsive or reckless in your pursuits.

May 19th marks the Mars conjunction with the True Node, symbolizing a turning point in your destiny. Pay attention to synchronicities and trust your instincts. It's a time for action, courage, and taking decisive steps towards your goals.

The month concludes with Mercury conjunct Uranus on May 31st, sparking innovative ideas and stimulating conversations. Embrace your unique perspective and share your thoughts with others. This alignment can bring unexpected insights and breakthroughs.

Love

In matters of love, May presents both challenges and opportunities for Taurus. The Venus square Pluto aspect on May 1st brings intensity and power struggles in relationships. It's crucial to address underlying issues and find a balance between asserting your needs and maintaining harmony.

The Venus sextile Saturn on May 13th and the Venus conjunction Uranus on May 18th bring stability and excitement to romantic partnerships. These alignments support deepening connections and creating a sense of security within relationships while also encouraging spontaneity and novelty.

Taurus singles may find themselves drawn to unconventional and unique individuals during this period. Embrace the opportunities for growth and exploration, but also maintain a sense of groundedness and stability in your interactions.

Career

Career-wise, May holds promise for Taurus. The Mars sextile Pluto aspect on May 3rd empowers you with determination and the ability to make significant strides in your professional endeavors. This alignment brings focus, ambition, and the drive to achieve your goals.

On May 10th, the Mars semi-square Uranus can bring unexpected changes or disruptions in the workplace. Adaptability and flexibility are key to navigating these shifts successfully. Embrace innovation and be open to new ideas or approaches.

The Sun conjunct Jupiter on May 18th brings opportunities for expansion, growth, and recognition. This alignment can open doors and bring positive developments in your career. Embrace new responsibilities and showcase your abilities with confidence.

Finance

In terms of finances, May requires cautious and practical financial management for Taurus. The Venus square Pluto on May 1st reminds you to be mindful of power dynamics in financial partnerships. Ensure that agreements are fair and transparent to avoid any potential disputes.

The Venus sextile Saturn on May 13th supports responsible financial planning and long-term stability. This alignment encourages you to set realistic goals, budget wisely, and focus on building a solid foundation for your financial future.

The Venus conjunction Uranus on May 18th brings opportunities for financial growth through unconventional means. Be open to unexpected financial prospects and innovative investment opportunities. However, assess risks carefully before making any major financial decisions.

Health

In terms of health, May reminds Taurus to prioritize self-care and emotional well-being. The Sun semi-square Neptune on May 3rd may create some emotional confusion or a need for retreat. Take time for relaxation, meditation, or engaging in activities that bring you inner peace.

The Mars conjunction Chiron on May 29th encourages you to address any emotional or physical wounds that may be impacting your well-being. Seek healing modalities, therapy, or engage in self-reflection to promote overall health and harmony.

Maintaining a balanced routine, regular exercise, and a healthy diet are essential during this period. Focus on activities that nurture your body, mind, and soul to maintain optimal well-being.

Travel

May presents opportunities for travel and exploration for Taurus. However, it's important to plan and prepare carefully due to potential unexpected changes or disruptions.

The Sun conjunct Jupiter on May 18th signals favorable conditions for travel, especially to unfamiliar destinations. Embrace new experiences and broaden your horizons through cultural immersion and adventurous activities.

However, with the Mars semi-square Uranus on May 10th, it's crucial to remain flexible and adaptable in your travel plans. Stay updated with travel advisories and be prepared for potential adjustments or delays.

Insight from the stars

May is a powerful month for Taurus, with a focus on personal growth, relationships, and financial stability. Take time for self-reflection, but also don't shy away from socializing and networking. Balance is key.

Best days of the month: May 3rd, 13th, 18th,19th, 23rd, 28th and 31st.

June 2024

Horoscope

June brings a dynamic mix of energies for Taurus, with opportunities for growth, introspection, and adjustments. The month begins with Mars semi-sextile Uranus on June 1st, infusing you with a burst of energy and the desire for change. This aspect encourages you to embrace your individuality and explore new possibilities.

The Sun quintile Neptune on June 1st enhances your intuition and spiritual connection. This alignment invites you to trust your inner guidance and tap into your creative potential.

Venus quintile Neptune on June 2nd deepens your sensitivity and compassion in matters of love and relationships. This aspect supports emotional connection and fosters understanding with your loved ones.

Mercury semi-square True Node on June 2nd emphasizes the importance of effective communication and meaningful connections. Pay attention to the information and messages that come your way, as they may offer guidance and insights regarding your life path.

The Jupiter trine Pluto on June 2nd empowers you with a renewed sense of purpose and the ability to transform your life. This alignment brings opportunities for growth, success, and personal evolution.

The Mercury sextile Neptune on June 2nd enhances your imaginative and creative abilities. It's an excellent time for artistic pursuits, spiritual exploration, and expressing your ideas with clarity and sensitivity.

The Sun sextile True Node on June 3rd highlights your ability to align with your true purpose and make positive connections with others. This aspect supports collaborative efforts and can bring helpful people into your life.

Love

In matters of love, June presents opportunities for deeper emotional connections and self-reflection for Taurus. The Sun and Venus conjunction on June 4th amplifies your magnetism and attractiveness, making you more alluring to others.

Mercury's trine to Pluto on June 4th intensifies your emotional depth and encourages meaningful conversations in relationships. This aspect promotes honesty, trust, and the sharing of profound experiences.

Venus square Saturn on June 8th may bring some challenges or limitations in love. It's crucial to approach relationship issues with patience, understanding, and a willingness to find common ground.

The Venus sextile Chiron on June 11th offers an opportunity for healing and growth within your relationships. It encourages vulnerability and the exploration of emotional wounds in order to foster deeper connections.

Career

In terms of career, June brings a mix of opportunities and challenges for Taurus. The Mars square Pluto on June 11th may bring power struggles or conflicts in the workplace. It's essential to maintain professionalism, assert healthy boundaries, and find diplomatic solutions.

The Venus square Saturn on June 8th may bring some financial limitations or delays in professional endeavors. Exercise caution with money matters and budget wisely during this period.

The Mercury sextile Mars on June 21st enhances your communication skills and assertiveness in professional situations. It's an excellent time for negotiations, presentations, and taking initiative in your career.

Finance

Financially, June calls for caution and practicality for Taurus. The Venus square Saturn on June 8th advises careful budgeting and responsible spending. It's crucial to assess your financial commitments and prioritize long-term stability.

The Mars semi-square Neptune on June 8th may bring some confusion or potential financial pitfalls. Be cautious with investments or major financial decisions during this period. Seek professional advice if needed.

Health

In terms of health, June reminds Taurus to focus on self-care and maintaining a balanced lifestyle. The Sun quintile Chiron on June 26th offers opportunities for healing and self-improvement. Explore alternative healing modalities and nurture your emotional well-being.

The Mars semi-square Neptune on June 29th may impact your energy levels and immune system. Prioritize rest, stress management, and healthy habits to support your overall well-being.

Travel

June presents favorable conditions for travel and exploration for Taurus. However, it's essential to plan and prepare carefully to ensure smooth experiences.

The Mercury sextile Uranus on June 29th encourages you to embrace spontaneity and seek unique travel opportunities. It's a great time for adventure, exploring new cultures, and connecting with people from different backgrounds.

Insight from the stars

June is a balanced month for Taurus, with opportunities in finance, relationships, and personal growth. The energies of the New Moon and the Sun in Gemini favor financial planning and communication.

Best days of the month: June 4th, 11th, 21st,26th, 29th, and 30th

July 2024

Horoscope

July brings a mix of energetic shifts and opportunities for growth for Taurus. As the month begins, the Jupiter semi-square Chiron on July 1st encourages you to confront any emotional wounds and seek healing. This aspect prompts self-reflection and personal growth.

Mercury's quintile Mars on July 1st enhances your mental agility and assertiveness. It's an excellent time for effective communication and taking decisive action in various areas of your life.

The Sun's semi-square Uranus on July 1st may bring unexpected changes or disruptions. It's important to remain adaptable and open to new possibilities during this time.

The Mercury trine Neptune on July 2nd heightens your intuition and imaginative abilities. It's an ideal period for spiritual exploration, creative pursuits, and deepening your connection to the mystical.

The Sun square True Node on July 2nd emphasizes the need to align with your true purpose and make decisions that are in harmony with your authentic self. It's a time to reassess your goals and make necessary adjustments.

Love

In matters of love, July encourages Taurus to focus on self-love and authentic connections. The Venus trine Saturn on July 2nd fosters stability and commitment in relationships. It's a favorable period for building strong foundations and deepening emotional bonds.

The Venus square Chiron on July 6th may bring up past wounds or insecurities in relationships. Use this time for healing and addressing any unresolved emotional issues with compassion and understanding.

Mercury's quintile Uranus on July 7th enhances your ability to express your unique ideas and opinions in relationships. It's a great time for open-minded conversations and embracing individuality within partnerships.

Career

Career-wise, July presents opportunities for growth and success for Taurus. The Mars sextile Saturn on July 5th brings a harmonious blend of discipline and ambition, allowing you to make steady progress toward your professional goals.

The Mercury sextile Jupiter on July 8th enhances your communication skills and intellectual abilities. This aspect supports networking, negotiations, and collaborative efforts in your career.

The Jupiter sextile True Node on July 9th brings positive energy and alignment with your life purpose. It's a time to embrace new opportunities and expand your horizons professionally.

Finance

Financially, July encourages Taurus to focus on practicality and long-term stability. The Venus trine Saturn on July 2nd supports wise financial decisions and responsible budgeting. It's a favorable time to assess your financial goals and make necessary adjustments.

The Venus sextile Uranus on July 8th brings opportunities for financial growth and innovation. Keep an open mind and be willing to explore new avenues for income and investment.

Health

In terms of health, July encourages Taurus to prioritize self-care and well-being. The Mars conjunction Uranus on July 15th may bring bursts of energy and motivation but also the need for balance and moderation. Avoid pushing yourself too hard and listen to your body's needs.

The Sun trine Saturn on July 10th supports discipline and consistency in maintaining a healthy lifestyle. It's an ideal time for establishing new routines and committing to self-improvement.

Travel

July presents favorable conditions for travel and exploration for Taurus. The Venus quintile Uranus on July 18th brings excitement and opportunities for unique experiences during your journeys. Embrace spontaneity and be open to new cultural experiences.

The Sun sextile Uranus on July 18th enhances your sense of adventure and encourages you to step out of your comfort zone. It's an excellent time to embark on spontaneous trips or try something new and exciting.

Insight from the stars

This July, the stars guide Taurus through a journey of emotional depth, creativity, and self-reflection. As the Sun enters Leo, it's time to unleash your creative side and pursue what makes your heart sing. Balance in all aspects of life is key this month.

Best days of the month: July 8th, 10th,15th,18th, 21st, 23rd, and 30th.

August 2024

Horoscope

August brings a mix of challenges and opportunities
for growth for Taurus. As the month begins, Mars
sextile True Node on August 1st energizes your social
interactions and encourages you to connect with like-
minded individuals who share your goals and
aspirations.

The Venus quintile Jupiter on August 2nd brings a
sense of optimism and expansion in love and
relationships. It's a favorable time to explore new
romantic possibilities or deepen existing connections.

However, the Venus square Uranus on August 2nd
may bring unexpected disruptions or changes in
relationships. It's important to remain adaptable and
open-minded during this period.

The Sun biquintile Saturn on August 4th promotes
discipline and practicality in various aspects of your
life. It's an ideal time for planning, organizing, and
making steady progress towards your goals.

In love, career, finances, health, and travel, August
presents both challenges and opportunities for growth.
It's a month that calls for adaptability, perseverance,
and self-reflection.

Love

In matters of love, August encourages Taurus to focus
on open communication and emotional healing. The
Venus square Neptune on August 4th may bring
confusion or idealization in relationships. It's essential
to maintain clarity and communicate honestly to
avoid misunderstandings.

The Venus biquintile True Node on August 6th
enhances your intuition and encourages you to trust
your instincts in matters of the heart. It's a favorable
time to make decisions that align with your soul's
growth.

The Sun sextile Jupiter on August 7th brings joy and
enthusiasm in romantic pursuits. It's an ideal period

for creating memorable experiences with your loved one or exploring new social activities where you can meet potential partners.

Career

Career-wise, August presents opportunities for growth and professional advancement for Taurus. The Mars conjunction Jupiter on August 14th brings a surge of energy and motivation to pursue your career goals and expand your horizons.

The Sun square Uranus on August 19th may bring unexpected changes or disruptions in your professional life. It's important to remain adaptable and open to new possibilities during this time.

The Jupiter square Saturn on August 19th calls for balance and moderation in your career endeavors. It's a time to assess your long-term goals and make necessary adjustments to achieve success.

Finance

Financially, August encourages Taurus to focus on responsible budgeting and strategic investments. The

Venus square Jupiter on August 19th may bring a temptation to overspend or make impulsive financial decisions. It's crucial to maintain a balanced approach and consider the long-term consequences of your actions.

The Venus trine Pluto on August 29th brings opportunities for financial transformation and growth. It's a favorable time to explore new investment opportunities or seek advice from trusted financial advisors.

Health

In terms of health, August emphasizes the importance of self-care and stress management for Taurus. The Sun sesquiquadrate Neptune on August 6th may bring emotional sensitivity and fatigue. It's crucial to prioritize rest and relaxation to maintain your physical and emotional well-being.

The Sun biquintile Pluto on August 28th enhances your ability to transform and heal on a deep level. It's a favorable time for incorporating new wellness practices or seeking alternative healing modalities.

Travel

August presents favorable conditions for travel and exploration for Taurus. The Venus trine Uranus on August 27th brings excitement and unique experiences during your journeys. Embrace spontaneity and be open to new cultural encounters.

The Sun biquintile Pluto on August 28th enhances your sense of adventure and encourages you to step out of your comfort zone. It's an excellent time to embark on solo adventures or connect with like-minded travelers.

Insight from the stars

This August, Taurus, embrace the change that comes your way and see it as an opportunity for growth. Remember to stay flexible and adaptable this month, and trust in your strength and resilience.

Best days of the month: August 6th, 14th, 19th, 22nd, 23rd, 28th and 30th.

September 2024

Horoscope

In September 2024, Taurus individuals can expect a mix of opportunities and challenges in various areas of life. The planetary aspects during this month will influence your love life, career, finances, health, and travel. It is important to stay grounded and make practical decisions to navigate through these influences.

The month begins with Mercury trine Chiron on September 2nd, promoting healing and communication. This aspect encourages Taurus to express their emotions and seek resolutions in relationships. Additionally, Mercury biquintile Neptune enhances your intuitive abilities, allowing you to tap into your subconscious mind for guidance.

On the same day, the Sun quintile Mars empowers you with vitality and assertiveness. You'll feel motivated to pursue your goals and make progress in your endeavors. However, be cautious as Mars square Neptune on September 3rd may bring confusion or misunderstandings. Take extra care in your communication and avoid making impulsive decisions.

The Sun sesquiquadrate Pluto on September 6th may bring some inner conflicts and power struggles within yourself. This aspect urges you to examine your motivations and address any self-limiting beliefs that may hinder your progress. Use this time for introspection and personal growth.

Mercury square Uranus on September 7th indicates a need for flexibility and adaptability in your communication. Unexpected changes or disruptions may arise, requiring you to think on your feet and find innovative solutions. Embrace the opportunity to break free from routine and explore new possibilities.

Love

The opposition between Venus and the True Node on September 3rd may bring relationship tensions to the surface. It's essential to address any underlying issues and communicate openly with your partner. Remember to find a balance between your personal desires and the needs of your relationship.

As the month progresses, Venus trine Jupiter on September 15th brings a harmonious and joyful energy to your love life. This aspect encourages romantic gestures, deepening the bond with your partner. It's an excellent time for romantic getaways or exploring shared interests together.

On September 16th, Venus opposes Chiron, which may bring up unresolved wounds or insecurities in your relationships. It's essential to approach these challenges with compassion and open-heartedness. Seek healing within yourself and support your partner's emotional well-being.

The month concludes with Venus sesquiquadrate Jupiter on September 27th, reminding you to maintain a healthy balance between love and personal growth. Avoid becoming overly dependent on your partner for happiness. Nurture your individuality and pursue your passions, as this will contribute positively to your relationship.

Career

Mars quincunx Pluto on September 4th may create power struggles or conflicts in the workplace. It's crucial to handle these situations with diplomacy and find common ground with colleagues and superiors. Focus on building alliances and fostering collaboration rather than asserting dominance.

The Sun sesquiquadrate Pluto on September 6th presents an opportunity for self-reflection and growth. Evaluate your motivations and address any self-limiting beliefs that may hinder your professional progress. Embrace your personal power and use it responsibly to achieve your goals.

Mercury square Uranus on September 7th indicates potential disruptions or sudden changes in your work environment. Adaptability and flexibility will be essential during this time. Embrace the opportunity to think outside the box and find innovative solutions to challenges that arise.

As the month progresses, Mercury quintile Mars on September 21st enhances your communication skills and assertiveness. It's an excellent time for presenting ideas, negotiating deals, or making important decisions. Your words will carry weight, so choose them wisely and assert yourself confidently.

Remember to balance your ambition with patience and diplomacy, as the Sun opposition Saturn on September 8th reminds you. Be cautious in making impulsive career moves or taking on unnecessary risks. Strategic planning and a step-by-step approach will yield better results in the long run.

Finance

Taurus individuals need to exercise caution and prudence in their financial matters during September 2024. The Sun opposition Saturn on September 8th urges you to assess your financial situation and make responsible choices. Avoid impulsive spending or risky investments. Focus on long-term stability rather than short-term gains.

The Venus trine Jupiter on September 15th brings a favorable energy to your financial sector. This aspect

may open doors for financial opportunities or bring
financial rewards. However, it's crucial to approach
these opportunities with discernment and avoid
overspending or overindulging.

Venus biquintile Saturn on September 15th
encourages you to find a balance between enjoying
the fruits of your labor and maintaining financial
discipline. Consider creating a budget or reevaluating
your financial goals during this time. Taking a
practical and strategic approach to your finances will
bring you stability and security in the long run.

During the latter part of the month, Venus
sesquiquadrate Jupiter on September 27th serves as a
reminder not to rely solely on material possessions or
external sources of happiness. True abundance comes
from within, and it's important to prioritize emotional
well-being over excessive materialism.

By maintaining financial discipline, making prudent
choices, and focusing on long-term stability, you can
navigate the financial challenges of September 2024
and set a solid foundation for your future financial
well-being.

Health

In September 2024, Taurus individuals should pay attention to their physical and mental well-being. Venus sesquiquadrate Uranus on September 8th reminds you to prioritize self-care and listen to your body's needs. Sudden changes or disruptions in your routine may impact your health, so it's crucial to maintain a balanced lifestyle.

Maintaining a healthy diet and regular exercise routine is especially important during this time. Establish a self-care practice that nurtures both your physical and emotional well-being. Consider incorporating activities like yoga, meditation, or spending time in nature to reduce stress and promote overall well-being.

Be mindful of any signs of burnout or excessive stress. If you find yourself feeling overwhelmed, take a step back and prioritize rest and relaxation. Remember that self-care is not selfish but necessary for your overall health and productivity.

Seeking emotional support from loved ones or a professional therapist can also be beneficial during this time. Sharing your feelings and concerns with others can help alleviate stress and provide fresh perspectives.

Remember to engage in activities that bring you joy and nourish your soul. Whether it's pursuing a hobby, spending time with loved ones, or indulging in creative outlets, prioritize activities that uplift your spirits and contribute positively to your mental well-being.

Lastly, practice mindfulness and self-compassion. Be patient with yourself as you navigate any health challenges that may arise. Celebrate your progress and achievements, no matter how small, and remember that your well-being is a journey, not a destination.

Travel

The Sun biquintile Chiron on September 8th encourages you to step out of your comfort zone and embrace new adventures. Whether it's a spontaneous day trip or a planned vacation, allow yourself to enjoy the journey and expand your horizons.

If you have been contemplating a trip, this is an excellent time to plan and make necessary arrangements. Consider exploring new destinations that resonate with your interests and offer opportunities for personal growth and cultural enrichment.

However, as with any travel plans, it's essential to stay informed about current travel restrictions, safety protocols, and health advisories. Be prepared for unexpected changes or disruptions in your travel plans and remain flexible.

During your travels, embrace the spirit of adventure and open-mindedness. Engage with the local culture, try new cuisines, and immerse yourself in new experiences. This is a time to broaden your horizons and create lasting memories.

Whether you're traveling solo, with a partner, or in a group, communication and compromise will be key. Ensure that everyone's needs and preferences are taken into consideration, allowing for a harmonious and enjoyable travel experience.

Remember to prioritize self-care during your travels. Take breaks, rest when needed, and maintain a balanced schedule to avoid exhaustion. Stay hydrated, eat nutritious meals, and practice good hygiene to safeguard your well-being.

Lastly, keep an open mind and embrace the unexpected. Travel often brings unforeseen adventures and serendipitous encounters. Allow yourself to be in the present moment and fully immerse yourself in the beauty and wonder of your chosen destinations.

Insight from the stars

This is a time of balance, self-reflection, and relationship building. In your career, relationships, health, and travels, seek harmony and be open to both giving and receiving. Stay grounded but allow yourself to dream. Trust your intuition and embrace the ebbs and flows of the month.

Best days of the month: September 2nd, 15th, 19th, 21st, 22nd, 26th and 30th.

October 2024

Horoscope

In October 2024, Taurus individuals can expect a month filled with transformative energies and opportunities for growth. The planetary aspects during this time will influence your love life, career, finances, health, and travel. It is important to embrace change, cultivate self-awareness, and make conscious choices to navigate through these influences.

Mercury's sesquiquadrate Uranus on October 2nd may bring unexpected changes or disruptions in communication. Be open to new ideas and be willing to adapt to different perspectives. Embrace the opportunity to break free from old patterns and embrace innovative solutions.

The influence of Venus throughout the month highlights themes of love and relationships. Venus' trine Saturn on October 4th brings stability and commitment to your love life. It is a favorable time for deepening your connection with your partner and solidifying your commitment.

Love

In matters of love, October 2024 holds transformative energies for Taurus individuals. Venus' influence throughout the month emphasizes deep connections, passion, and personal growth within relationships.

The sesquiquadrate aspect between Venus and Neptune on October 3rd brings a heightened sensitivity and emotional depth to your love life. It's a time to connect on a spiritual and intuitive level with your partner. Pay attention to your dreams, as they may hold symbolic messages related to your relationship.

Venus' trine Saturn on October 4th brings stability and commitment to your love life. This aspect strengthens the foundations of your relationship and encourages open communication, trust, and shared responsibilities. It's an excellent time for making long-term plans and setting mutual goals with your partner.

On October 8th, Venus trine Mars enhances passion, sensuality, and harmonious interactions in your romantic relationships. This aspect deepens your connection and fosters a sense of mutual understanding and support. Enjoy intimate moments and express your love and desire openly with your partner.

However, Mercury's opposition to Chiron on October 8th may bring up past wounds or insecurities in relationships. It's essential to approach these challenges with empathy, understanding, and patience. Take the opportunity to heal past wounds and deepen your emotional connection with your partner.

Throughout the month, be open to exploring new depths of intimacy and vulnerability in your relationships. Trust your instincts and allow your heart to guide you. Embrace the transformative energies and communicate your needs, desires, and fears with your partner.

Career

October 2024 presents both challenges and opportunities in your career, Taurus. It's essential to maintain a diplomatic approach and make wise decisions to navigate through these influences successfully.

Mercury's square Mars on October 6th may bring communication challenges or conflicts in the workplace. It's crucial to remain calm and composed when dealing with colleagues or superiors. Practice active listening and choose your words wisely to avoid misunderstandings or unnecessary confrontations.

The biquintile aspect between Mercury and Uranus on October 7th enhances your innovative thinking and problem-solving abilities. Embrace the opportunity to think outside the box and find creative solutions to challenges that arise. Your unique ideas and perspectives can bring a fresh approach to your work.

On October 8th, Mercury's trine Jupiter amplifies your communication skills and intellectual capabilities. This aspect promotes collaboration and networking opportunities, enabling you to expand your professional connections. It's an excellent time for presentations, negotiations, or engaging in intellectual pursuits.

However, Mercury's opposition to Chiron on October 8th may trigger self-doubt or insecurities related to your career. Remember to have confidence in your abilities and seek support or guidance from mentors or trusted colleagues. Use this time for personal growth and self-reflection to overcome any limiting beliefs.

Finance

October 2024 requires Taurus individuals to exercise caution and prudence in their financial matters. It's crucial to make conscious choices and seek expert advice to navigate through the influences of the month successfully.

Venus' opposition to Uranus on October 14th may bring unexpected financial changes or expenses. It's important to have a contingency plan and be prepared for any unforeseen circumstances. Avoid impulsive spending and focus on maintaining financial stability and security.

On October 17th, Venus' sextile Pluto brings opportunities for financial growth and empowerment. This aspect may open doors for increased income or favorable investments. However, exercise caution and conduct thorough research before making significant financial decisions. Seek advice from financial experts or professionals if needed.

Mercury's opposition to Uranus on October 30th may introduce financial uncertainties or disruptions. It's essential to remain adaptable and flexible in your financial strategies. Keep a close eye on your budget and prioritize long-term financial goals over short-term gains.

During this month, avoid unnecessary risks or impulsive investments. Instead, focus on creating a solid financial foundation and exploring stable and reliable avenues for growth. Maintain a balanced approach to your finances and seek opportunities for increasing your savings or reducing debt.

Consider reviewing your financial plans and budget during October. Look for areas where you can make adjustments or cut unnecessary expenses. Keep track of your financial transactions and seek ways to optimize your resources.

By being proactive and conscious in your financial decisions, you can navigate the challenges of October

2024 and set a strong foundation for long-term financial stability and growth.

Health

The biquintile aspect between Venus and Chiron on October 15th emphasizes the need for emotional healing and self-nurturing. Pay attention to your emotional well-being and engage in activities that bring you joy and inner peace. Practice self-compassion and allow yourself to rest and recharge when needed.

The Sun's biquintile Neptune on October 26th encourages holistic well-being and spiritual practices. Consider incorporating activities such as meditation, yoga, or mindfulness into your daily routine. Connect with your inner self and nurture your spiritual side to promote overall balance and harmony.

Maintaining a healthy lifestyle is crucial during this time. Focus on nourishing your body with nutritious meals, regular exercise, and sufficient rest. Establish a consistent sleep schedule and create a calming bedtime routine to improve the quality of your sleep.

It's important to manage stress effectively as well. Identify stress triggers and find healthy coping mechanisms to reduce its impact on your overall well-being. Engage in activities that help you unwind, such as reading, listening to music, or spending time in nature.

Don't hesitate to seek professional support if needed. Whether it's consulting a therapist, nutritionist, or personal trainer, reaching out for guidance can provide valuable insights and support on your journey to optimal health.

Remember that self-care is not selfish but essential for your overall well-being. Prioritize self-care activities that replenish your energy and promote a positive mindset. By taking care of yourself physically, mentally, and emotionally, you'll be better equipped to handle the challenges and embrace the opportunities that October brings.

Travel

On October 6th, Mercury square Mars may create some tension or disruptions in your travel plans. It's crucial to stay adaptable and be prepared for unexpected changes or challenges. Have backup plans and remain flexible to ensure smooth travels.

As the month progresses, Mercury trine Jupiter on October 8th enhances your communication skills and brings a positive energy to your travel experiences. It's an excellent time for cultural exchanges, meeting new people, or exploring new destinations. Embrace the opportunities for growth and learning during your travels.

However, be mindful of potential misunderstandings or miscommunications as Mercury opposes Chiron on October 8th. Clear and open communication will be essential to navigate any challenges that arise during your travels. Practice patience and understanding, both with yourself and others.

On October 22nd, Venus trine True Node encourages meaningful and fated travel experiences. Pay attention to synchronicities and trust in the divine guidance that leads you to new destinations or encounters. Embrace the spirit of adventure and allow yourself to be open to unexpected discoveries.

Overall, October 2024 presents opportunities for Taurus individuals to embark on travel adventures and expand their horizons. Stay adaptable, embrace new experiences, and approach your travels with a sense of curiosity and wonder.

Insight from the stars

October is a month of transformation for Taurus. This is a time to embrace change, both in your personal and professional life. Harness the balanced energy of Libra to build harmonious relationships and use the penetrating energy of Scorpio to delve into the depths of your soul. Be open, be brave, and be ready to transform.

Best days of the month: October 8th, 13th, 17th, 22nd, 25th, 28th and 31st

November 2024

Horoscope

In November 2024, Taurus individuals can expect a month of transformation, growth, and spiritual exploration. The planetary aspects influence various areas of your life, urging you to embrace change, pursue personal development, and align with your higher purpose.

Jupiter sextile Chiron on November 2nd brings opportunities for healing and self-discovery. This aspect encourages you to confront any emotional wounds or limiting beliefs that may be holding you back. Seek out spiritual practices, therapy, or self-reflection to support your personal growth journey.

Mercury trine Mars on November 2nd enhances your mental clarity and communication skills. It's an excellent time for expressing your ideas, engaging in intellectual pursuits, or pursuing educational opportunities. Use this energy to assert yourself confidently and make progress in your endeavors.

Venus opposition Jupiter on November 3rd may bring some conflicts or challenges in your relationships or partnerships. It's important to find a balance between your individual needs and the needs of others. Practice open and honest communication to address any issues and seek compromises.

As the month progresses, the Sun trine Saturn on November 4th brings stability and discipline to your life. This aspect encourages you to focus on long-term goals and make practical decisions that support your personal and professional growth. Embrace structure and responsibility as you navigate your path.

Mercury square Saturn on November 12th may create some obstacles or delays in your plans. It's crucial to stay patient and persistent in pursuing your goals. Take this time to reassess your strategies and find innovative solutions to any challenges that arise.

The Sun opposition Uranus on November 16th brings
unexpected changes or disruptions in your life. It's
important to stay adaptable and embrace the
opportunities that arise from these shifts. Be open to
new experiences and trust in your ability to navigate
change.

As the month draws to a close, the Sun trine Neptune
on November 18th enhances your intuition and
spiritual connection. This aspect invites you to
explore your inner world, engage in meditation or
creative practices, and tap into your higher
consciousness. Trust your instincts and embrace the
wisdom that comes from within.

Overall, November 2024 is a transformative and
spiritually charged month for Taurus individuals.
Embrace personal growth, navigate challenges with
resilience, and stay open to the possibilities that arise.
By aligning with your higher purpose, you can create
a meaningful and fulfilling path forward.

Love

In November 2024, Taurus individuals may experience shifts and growth in their love lives. The planetary aspects influence your relationships, urging you to embrace authenticity, deepen connections, and nurture emotional bonds.

Venus opposition Jupiter on November 3rd may create some conflicts or challenges in your relationships. It's important to find a balance between your individual desires and the needs of your partner. Practice open and honest communication to address any issues and find compromises that support both parties.

The Sun trine Saturn on November 4th brings stability and commitment to your romantic relationships. This aspect encourages you to build a solid foundation based on trust, loyalty, and shared values. It's an excellent time for deepening commitments, making long-term plans, or taking your relationship to the next level.

However, be cautious of potential disruptions or sudden changes as the Sun opposes Uranus on November 16th. This aspect may bring unexpected shifts or conflicts in your love life. It's important to stay adaptable and approach any challenges with patience and understanding.

As the month progresses, the Sun trine Neptune on November 18th enhances the romantic and compassionate aspects of your relationships. This aspect invites you to deepen your emotional connection and express your love in heartfelt ways. Nurture the spiritual and soulful dimensions of your partnerships.

Career

In November 2024, Taurus individuals can expect significant developments and opportunities in their careers. The planetary aspects influence your professional life, bringing growth, recognition, and new pathways for success.

Jupiter sextile Chiron on November 2nd encourages you to explore your unique talents and pursue personal development in your career. Embrace opportunities for learning, skill enhancement, or expanding your professional network. This aspect supports your growth and boosts your confidence in the workplace.

Mercury trine Mars on November 2nd enhances your communication and assertiveness in professional settings. It's an excellent time for expressing your ideas, negotiating contracts, or engaging in strategic planning. Use this energy to make progress in your career goals and assert yourself confidently.

The Sun trine Saturn on November 4th brings stability and discipline to your professional life. This aspect encourages you to focus on long-term goals, establish solid foundations, and make practical decisions that support your advancement. Embrace responsibility and take on leadership roles with confidence.

Mercury square Saturn on November 12th may bring some challenges or delays in your career plans. It's important to stay patient and persistent, even in the face of obstacles. Use this time to reassess your strategies, make necessary adjustments, and find innovative solutions to any setbacks.

As the month progresses, the Sun trine Neptune on November 18th enhances your intuition and creativity in the workplace. This aspect invites you to tap into your inner wisdom, trust your instincts, and bring innovative ideas to the table. Embrace your unique perspective and contribute your creative talents to your professional endeavors.

Finance

In November 2024, Taurus individuals may experience shifts and opportunities in their financial situation. The planetary aspects influence your financial sector, encouraging stability, resourcefulness, and wise financial management.

Venus opposition Jupiter on November 3rd may bring some financial conflicts or challenges. It's important to find a balance between your desires for material abundance and the need for financial responsibility. Practice mindful spending, budgeting, and seek opportunities for financial growth that align with your long-term goals.

The Sun trine Saturn on November 4th brings stability and discipline to your financial affairs. This aspect encourages you to establish solid foundations, make practical decisions, and focus on long-term financial goals. Embrace responsible financial management and consider investments or savings plans that support your future financial security.

Be cautious of unexpected changes or disruptions as the Sun opposes Uranus on November 16th. This aspect may bring unforeseen expenses or fluctuations in your financial situation. It's crucial to stay adaptable and have contingency plans to navigate any financial challenges that arise.

As the month progresses, the Sun trine Neptune on November 18th enhances your intuition and creativity in financial matters. This aspect invites you to trust your instincts when making financial decisions and to explore innovative approaches to wealth accumulation. Embrace opportunities for spiritual and intuitive investments or ventures.

Health

In November 2024, Taurus individuals are encouraged to prioritize their physical and emotional well-being. The planetary aspects influence your health sector, urging you to embrace self-care, balance, and holistic approaches to wellness.

Jupiter sextile Chiron on November 2nd supports your healing journey and personal growth in all aspects of life, including health. Embrace practices that promote physical and emotional well-being, such as mindfulness, meditation, or holistic therapies. Seek out opportunities for self-reflection and personal transformation.

The Sun trine Saturn on November 4th brings discipline and stability to your health routines. This aspect encourages you to establish healthy habits, set realistic goals, and prioritize self-care. Embrace a balanced approach to your physical and emotional well-being, ensuring that you have time for rest, nourishment, and exercise.

However, be cautious of potential disruptions or sudden changes as the Sun opposes Uranus on November 16th. This aspect may bring unexpected health issues or disruptions in your routines. It's important to stay adaptable and approach any challenges with patience and a willingness to seek alternative solutions.

As the month progresses, the Sun trine Neptune on November 18th enhances your intuition and spiritual connection to your well-being. This aspect invites you to explore holistic and intuitive approaches to health. Embrace practices that nourish your soul, such as meditation, energy healing, or connecting with nature.

Travel

In November 2024, Taurus individuals may experience opportunities and shifts in their travel plans. The planetary aspects influence your travel

sector, encouraging exploration, expansion, and
cultural experiences.

Venus opposition Jupiter on November 3rd may bring
some challenges or conflicts related to travel. It's
important to find a balance between your desire for
adventure and the need for practicality. Consider
budgeting, planning, and communication to ensure
smooth travel experiences and avoid unnecessary
complications.

The Sun trine Saturn on November 4th brings stability
and discipline to your travel plans. This aspect
encourages you to make practical decisions, prioritize
safety and organization, and embrace responsible
travel habits. Whether it's for business or pleasure,
approach your travel with a sense of structure and
preparation.

As the month progresses, the Sun trine Neptune on
November 18th enhances your intuitive connection to
your travel experiences. This aspect invites you to
embrace the spiritual and transformative aspects of
your journeys. Allow yourself to be open to new
cultures, experiences, and connections, and trust your
instincts in choosing the right destinations and
activities.

Insight from the stars

November is a transformative month for Taurus. The
energies of Scorpio and Sagittarius combine to create
a period of deep introspection followed by expansion
and exploration. Pay attention to your dreams and
intuition, as they may reveal important insights.

Best days of the month: November 2nd, 4th, 12th,
18th, 21st, 23rd and 27th

December 2024

Horoscope

In December 2024, Taurus individuals will experience a mix of energies that will shape their overall general horoscope. The planetary aspects influence various areas of life, bringing opportunities, challenges, and transformative experiences.

Venus biquintile Jupiter on December 1st brings harmonious and expansive energies to your relationships and personal growth. This aspect encourages you to embrace joy, love, and positive experiences. Focus on cultivating meaningful connections and nurturing your existing relationships.

The Sun square Saturn on December 4th may present some obstacles or restrictions in your path. This aspect urges you to stay grounded, disciplined, and focused on your long-term goals. Be patient and persistent in overcoming any challenges that arise during this time.

Venus sextile Neptune on December 4th enhances your creativity, intuition, and spiritual connection. This aspect invites you to explore your artistic side and embrace activities that bring you joy and fulfillment. Use your imagination to manifest your desires and bring beauty into your life.

As the month progresses, the Sun opposition Jupiter on December 7th brings a sense of expansion and abundance. This aspect encourages you to broaden your horizons, seek new opportunities, and embrace a positive mindset. Trust in your abilities and have faith that the universe is supporting your growth.

On December 19th, Venus trine Jupiter enhances your social life and brings opportunities for growth and happiness. This aspect encourages you to embrace new friendships, expand your social circle, and engage in activities that bring you joy. It's a favorable time to network, collaborate, and seek support from others.

The Sun square Neptune on December 18th may bring some confusion or uncertainty. It's important to maintain clarity and focus during this time. Avoid making impulsive decisions or taking on unnecessary risks. Trust your intuition and seek guidance from your inner wisdom to navigate any challenges that arise.

As the month comes to an end, the Sun semi-sextile Pluto on December 21st invites you to embrace personal transformation and empowerment. This aspect brings intensity and a desire for inner growth. Use this energy to release what no longer serves you and embrace your personal power.

Overall, December 2024 presents a combination of opportunities and challenges for Taurus individuals. Embrace expansion, joy, and positive relationships while staying grounded, disciplined, and focused on your long-term goals. Trust your intuition, seek support when needed, and embrace personal growth and transformation.

Love

In December 2024, Taurus individuals will experience a mix of energies in their love life. The planetary aspects influence your relationships and romantic encounters, bringing both harmony and challenges.

Venus trine Uranus on December 2nd sparks excitement and a desire for freedom in your love life. This aspect may bring unexpected encounters or opportunities for romantic adventures. Embrace spontaneity and allow yourself to explore new experiences and connections.

The Sun conjunction Mercury on December 5th enhances communication and intellectual connection in your relationships. This aspect encourages open and honest conversations, allowing you to deepen your understanding and connection with your partner. It's a favorable time for expressing your thoughts, desires, and concerns.

However, be cautious of potential conflicts or misunderstandings as Venus square Mars on December 12th brings some tension and clashes in romantic relationships. It's important to practice patience, compromise, and open communication to overcome any challenges that arise. Avoid impulsive actions or words that may escalate conflicts.

Venus sextile Chiron on December 23rd brings opportunities for healing and growth in your love life. This aspect encourages you to embrace vulnerability, open your heart, and address any emotional wounds or barriers that may be affecting your relationships. It's a favorable time for seeking couples therapy or engaging in self-reflection to foster deeper connections.

Career

The Sun square Saturn on December 4th may present some challenges and obstacles in your career path. It's essential to stay focused, disciplined, and committed to your long-term goals during this time. Use this aspect as an opportunity to review your strategies, improve your skills, and develop a solid foundation for future success.

Venus sextile Neptune on December 4th enhances your creativity and intuition in the workplace. This aspect encourages you to infuse your work with artistic flair and imaginative solutions. Trust your instincts and explore innovative approaches to your tasks and projects. Your ability to blend practicality with creativity will impress others and open doors for advancement.

The Sun opposition Jupiter on December 7th brings opportunities for expansion and abundance in your career. This aspect encourages you to take calculated risks, explore new ventures, and embrace a positive mindset. Trust in your abilities and seek out opportunities for professional growth. Networking and collaborating with others can lead to exciting prospects and advancement.

On December 19th, Venus trine Jupiter enhances your professional relationships and brings positive interactions with colleagues and superiors. This aspect fosters cooperation, support, and recognition. It's a favorable time to showcase your talents, share your ideas, and seek guidance and mentorship from those in higher positions. Building strong alliances and leveraging your network will contribute to your career success.

Overall, December presents a combination of challenges and opportunities in your career. Stay focused, disciplined, and committed to your long-term goals. Embrace creativity, trust your instincts, and explore innovative approaches to your work. Seek out opportunities for expansion and collaboration, and nurture positive relationships with colleagues and superiors. Your dedication and strategic efforts will lead to professional growth and advancement.

Finance

The Sun square Saturn on December 4th may bring some financial challenges and limitations. It's important to exercise caution and discipline in your spending habits during this time. Stick to a budget, prioritize essential expenses, and avoid unnecessary splurges or risky investments. Patience and long-term planning will be key to financial stability.

Venus sextile Neptune on December 4th enhances your intuitive understanding of financial matters. This aspect encourages you to trust your instincts when making financial decisions. Listen to your inner guidance and rely on your creative problem-solving skills to identify opportunities for financial growth and stability.

The Sun opposition Jupiter on December 7th brings opportunities for financial expansion and abundance. This aspect encourages you to be open to new avenues of income and to explore investments or ventures that align with your long-term goals. However, exercise caution and thorough research before committing to any financial opportunities.

On December 19th, Venus trine Jupiter brings positive financial prospects and opportunities for growth. This aspect enhances your ability to attract abundance and material success. It's a favorable time to seek out financial advice or engage in strategic financial planning. Embrace opportunities for collaboration or partnerships that can lead to increased financial stability and prosperity.

Health

The Sun square Saturn on December 4th may bring some physical or mental challenges. Take this aspect as a reminder to slow down, rest, and address any health concerns that require attention. Prioritize self-care practices such as proper sleep, nutrition, and exercise. Implement stress-management techniques to maintain overall well-being.

Venus sextile Neptune on December 4th enhances your emotional and mental health. This aspect encourages you to prioritize self-love, self-compassion, and nurturing activities. Engage in activities that bring you joy, relaxation, and peace of mind. Practice mindfulness, meditation, or engage in creative outlets to maintain emotional balance.

The Sun opposition Jupiter on December 7th can bring a tendency to overindulge or neglect healthy habits. Be mindful of excessive behaviors, whether related to food, drink, or other areas of self-care. Find a balance between enjoying the pleasures of life and maintaining a healthy routine. Seek opportunities for physical activities that bring joy and contribute to your overall well-being.

On December 19th, Venus trine Jupiter enhances your overall vitality and well-being. This aspect encourages a positive outlook and boosts your energy levels. Take advantage of this period to engage in activities that support your physical health and rejuvenation. Practice self-care rituals that promote relaxation, balance, and self-nurturing.

Travel

In December 2024, Taurus individuals will experience a mix of influences when it comes to

travel. While there may be some disruptions or
challenges, there are also opportunities for exciting
adventures and meaningful experiences.

The Sun square Saturn on December 4th may bring
some obstacles or delays in your travel plans. It's
important to be patient and flexible during this time.
Have contingency plans in place and be prepared for
potential changes or rescheduling. Use this period to
review your travel itineraries, ensure all necessary
documents are in order, and make necessary
adjustments.

Venus sextile Neptune on December 4th enhances
your travel experiences with a touch of magic and
inspiration. This aspect encourages you to seek out
destinations that resonate with your dreams and
desires. Embrace the opportunity to immerse yourself
in different cultures, indulge in culinary delights, and
connect with the beauty of your surroundings. Engage
in activities that promote relaxation and rejuvenation
during your travels.

The Sun opposition Jupiter on December 7th brings
opportunities for expansive and adventurous travel
experiences. This aspect encourages you to step
outside your comfort zone and explore new
destinations or embark on exciting journeys. Embrace
the spirit of adventure, connect with locals, and
immerse yourself in unique experiences. However, be

mindful of overspending or overindulgence during your travels.

On December 19th, Venus trine Jupiter enhances your travel experiences by fostering positive connections and opportunities for cultural exchange. This aspect encourages you to engage with others, seek out authentic experiences, and embrace the beauty of different cultures. Embrace opportunities for personal growth, self-discovery, and expanding your horizons through travel.

Insight from the stars

December is a month of celebration, reflection, and planning for Taurus. Embrace the adventurous Sagittarius energy at the start of the month and then transition into the focused Capricorn energy. The stars whisper that this month is a culmination of a year's journey; embrace it with open arms and a heart full of gratitude.

Best days of the month: December 2nd, 8th, 10th, 19th, 21st, 24th and 31st